"OH GOD,
MY HUSBAND IS
GAY"

"OH GOD, MY HUSBAND IS GAY"

Mariana G LoLon

authorHOUSE®

AuthorHouse™
1663 Liberty Drive
Bloomington, IN 47403
www.authorhouse.com
Phone: 1-800-839-8640

Published by AuthorHouse   06/10/2013

ISBN: 978-1-4817-5676-1 (sc)
ISBN: 978-1-4817-5675-4 (e)

Library of Congress Control Number: 2013909860

Contents

Dedications

Grandmother Emelia

My children

Grandchildren for their unconditional love

Special thanks to Anna for her contribution in helping me with editing and support as a friend.

MY JOURNEY

O n a long drive home one day I started to reminisce. The past came to mind. My fondest memories as well as my saddest. I wondered that day how time had passed so quickly in my life. I recalled my first kiss from my childhood sweetheart, dancing with my dad, my wedding day, and seeing my babies for the first time. These are just a few that came to mind. The saddest was the day my husband admitted he was gay, the death of my grandmother, and my son during a war not knowing his location. I had asked myself at one time if I had accomplished all I wanted to do and thought maybe not. Now I can say "yes, I have," and continue to do God's will. Like writing this book. I felt a need inside of me to write my story. If you have chosen this book to read, I hope it will give you new insight and benefit you or someone with a similar story like mine.

If you're taking this journey with me as you read, you might want to write in a notebook your thoughts and feelings. A bible, a prayer book might come in handy or even a picture. I often look at my grandmother's picture for courage and wisdom as I write. I read from time to time a passage from the bible.

Psalm 130:5. "I trust in the Lord: my soul trusts in His word." I have traveled many roads, smooth and bumpy. As much as I would have liked to take certain people with me on my journey, I learned I had to do it alone with God.

My husband is gay. It was not so easy at one time in my life to say that statement. I went through many phases to reach this point. This is my story and how I survived. I was married for thirty-five years when I discovered my husband was gay. At that time I had no one to relate to or understand. All I knew was that when my husband admitted to me he was gay, my life changed drastically.

There are five stages of grief. Denial, anger, bargaining, depression, and acceptance. Grief can occur to anyone who has experienced a loss. Throughout my book you will read how I experienced and dealt with the five stages. The stages are not necessary in any order or have a time limit. It's different for every person.

Chapter 2

CHILDHOOD HISTORY

S o I'll start from the beginning with my history. I was born in Chicago and an only child. My parents were Latin American. My father worked hard on ships and brought his parents, brothers, and two sisters to America. As far as I can remember, I was always told I was pretty, special, and had the biggest brown eyes. My grandparents on my father's side thought of me in this way and treated me like I was a princess. I remember sitting on my grandfather's lap and he would tell me how I was going to one day represent our family in a big way. I was going to make the family proud. I was destined to make a difference in our generation. My grandparents and father had struggled and worked hard all their life. It was rough at times he told me. America would give us a better life he said. I smiled and agreed. I must have been at least five. I really didn't understand but just agreeing made him happy. That's all that mattered to me. My grandmother would smile at me too and tell me to just be myself. At a young age I thought to make others happy all I had to do was just go along with whatever they said.

My mother's family came from a different life style. My mother was the only daughter with two brothers. Her family was wealthy. She attended the best of schools and everything was given to her. My father spent a lot of time at sea. He worked very hard to earn money. He supported his parents and helped with his siblings as well. My mother left her family at a young age to get married. My mother was a stay-at-home mom during my childhood days.

My parents started having marital problems early on in their marriage. Even as a child, I can still remember hearing their yelling at each other from my bedroom. I spent a lot of my time in my bedroom pretending everything was normal.

My dad spent most of my growing up years at sea. When he did come home, it felt like Christmas morning for me. He always had a handful of presents for me. While he was home we always spent one day of quality time together. If it was a school day, I didn't attend at least that day. He would take me to baseball games to see a game if it was the season. Other times we went to his office aboard the ship he was working.

I looked forward to those times. I would sit at his desk and play with the typewriter. I would pretend I was in charge of the ship and he would play along. Then we would tour the ship. He'd proudly show me off. The cook would fix me whatever I wanted to eat. My dad made a point of letting me know how much he loved me just by his smile and attention.

To think I was told the day I was born he was disappointed because I wasn't a boy. Not anymore. I was daddy's little girl. He spoiled me whenever I was with him. When he was at sea he sent postcards from different places all over the world, and flowers for special occasions. He never forgot my birthday. When I was little, I use to pretend I was traveling with him. I thought my dad was the most perfect man in the world. In later years alcohol became a problem for him. It was a disappointment for me but I still continued to love him and he continued to spoil me. For a long time I didn't admit he had a problem. I just ignored the situation. I didn't want to believe my dad had flaws.

I also spent many special times with cousins from my dad's side of the family. Two of my cousins were like sisters to me. Our relationship became stronger throughout the years. I remember the Thanksgivings we shared together just dancing, laughing and telling stories.

My mother and I were not close. She did the motherly things as best she could, like taking me to school and trying to help me with my homework. Her English was not good and she had a difficult time helping me with homework. She often told me I would learn eventually on my own. I wish the nuns could have been more understanding. I struggled in school in my early years. I remember my mom being sad more than happy. I thought maybe it was because she missed her family in Santo Domingo.

My mother's time with me was limited. I often wished we could be closer. Once in a while we went to a movie, or she took me shopping for clothes and groceries. I spent more time with my grandmother, my dad's mom. My mother seemed to enjoy mostly spending time with friends. Sometimes I thought I was an inconvenience to her. I now think she was too young and didn't know how to raise a child. My mom was only seventeen when she got married and dad was thirty. Thankfully, I was brought up in the Catholic faith and attended a Catholic School.

We traveled the summers to Santo Domingo to visit my mother's family. Her parents were divorced so I divided my time with them. I didn't always feel comfortable with them like I did with my dad's family. My mother's family was more prominent. Their values were different. Money was more important. I did enjoy my great-grandmother. She was different and full of life. She enjoyed music. She told me at one time she was a flamingo dancer. She also played the cassanetts and taught me how to play. She tried showing me dancing too but she would lose her balance. She was ninety at the time with quite a sense of humor.

I lived a very sheltered life. Family was all I knew. At school I was shy and had few friends. My aunt and grandmother lived on a street referred as "the block" in Chicago, a west side story atmosphere. Everyone knew who you were and I felt safe there. I spent most of my growing up years with my grandmother and cousins. I had some fun times with them. My cousins and I would jump rope, dress up, and talk about boys. I met my first love when I was about thirteen. Secretively of course. He was from the "block."

We use to stay on the phone as long as we could. He would walk me home sometimes on a summer evening with my cousin. He gave me my first kiss. We went together on and off through high school. We even had our own special bench in the park. It was a special time in my life. I thought we would one day get married. God had other plans for me.

I spent most of my time with my dad's mom. My grandmother was a caring person with a strong faith. She possessed a terrific sense of humor and told me old family stories. I'm proud to say that I inherited my values from her. My grandmother showed me the ways God loved others and me. She helped me to make the right choices during my difficult teenage years.

My parents separated when I was a teenager. I was constantly in the middle of who should raise me. I told myself from that point on, that my life would be different. I would make sure my children would one day have a better life. After my dad retired, I moved to the Cayman Islands with him and my grandmother. I loved living in the islands.

The beaches were beautiful. The water was so blue and clear. I would spend time at the beach almost every day. My dad went back to sea temporarily. My grandmother was like my best friend. We did everything together. We went to movies, grocery shopping, and ate dinner together. I could talk to her about any subject. I went to work but continued to spend time with my grandmother. She often told me I should be with people my own age, and she encouraged me to date. I would tell her, "I have plenty of time to date." "Besides you're more fun." She would smile. I eventually did date but no one seemed to interest me. It wasn't all that important.

Chapter 3

ENCOUNTERED LOVE

Every girl believes at one time or another in fairytales. I met my prince charming in the Cayman Islands. He was in the military. He was a blind date. I have to say that when we met, it was love at first sight for me. We dated and talked on the phone for hours. He was cute, smart, and had a great personality. When he smiled at me my heart seemed to skip a beat.

It wasn't long before we were engaged and planning to move to the states where he was born and grew up in a small town. As I left my grandmother I felt sad. She, however, was happy for me and fond of my fiancée. "Time for you to start a new life, "she had told me. "I will always be with you" she added. Dad was not happy. He offered me a new car if I wouldn't get married. I knew it was his way of saying he would miss me. When I said goodbye to my dad he just held me close not facing me and walked away. At the time I was so filled with emotions pertaining to me, I didn't respond to my dad.

A new chapter began in my life. I had moved to a new state with a different culture. The food was different too. My new in-laws were nice to me. I fell in love with my father-in-law instantly. I felt comfortable with him. He'd spend time with me talking, and telling me about their family stories. He taught me about his culture and how to find and catch crawfish which was not appealing to me. My father-in-law gave me my first driving lesson in his pickup truck.

Married life was great in the beginning. Later it became filled with challenges. I was getting acclimated to a different location, as well as making adjustments, and then I became pregnant. Our first son was born on my father's birthday. He was beautiful. He had the biggest brown eyes but so tiny. He was born pre-mature. As I held him in my arms for the first time, I just knew he would be a survivor. He stayed in the hospital till he gained the necessary weight to come home. What a happy day it was the day he came home.

We had many sleepless nights. He was a sick little baby but always pulled through like a champ. I could always count on my husband to help. We had a beautiful daughter two years later and another son born on my father-in-laws birthday. I had two proud grandfathers.

Our children became our life. There were times of sickness, laughter, and growth. I cherished being a mom. I went to work to help with our children's education. A Catholic education was important to my husband and me. Our lives became busy with work, homework, and extra-curricular activities. We were active in our church. We gave Engaged Encounter weekends, Marriage Encounters, and served in other ministries. As busy as our lives were, we managed to take time out for us too. It was usually a dinner out or a weekend away. My friends often told me my husband was the best husband of the group. I would smile to myself. I felt so fortunate and thankful.

I attended a yearly woman's retreat and when I returned home, my husband had dinner cooked and flowers for me. He told me how much he missed me. He often called my office, and asked my receptionist, "Can I speak to the woman of my life?" Every anniversary was special. It was a surprise trip or special dinner. I remember one year for our anniversary going to Arizona. We had a special dinner and went from lounge to lounge for someone to play our song. I never doubted his love. He was everything to me and more. In many ways he reminded me of my dad, always going the extra mile.

Years later my grandmother came to live with us. She was such a blessing to our family. I was so happy we were together again. I'd watch her saying her rosary and crocheting. I was soon back to telling her all about my day. She would listen and gave me positive advice. I was glad to be able to take care of her. My youngest son learned from her wisdom and compassion. His profession today deals with the elderly. At the time my husband was doing well with his employment. We had a comfortable home. We were involved in church ministries. We had a social life. We had good friends. All was well. Life couldn't be better and our children were doing well. Another chapter ended and a new one began.

Chapter 4

Disaster

Here it was a year later. It was another hot and humid day in July. I was driving home from work and thinking I couldn't wait to get home and change into some cooler clothes. The air conditioner in the car was on full blast, and it still didn't feel cool enough.

I recalled the year when my husband lost his job unexpectedly. I felt confused and helpless. Plans for the future had to be put on hold. I knew I loved him and I would help him through this difficult time. I was faced with going back to work. Change again entered my life. God would see us through I told myself.

I found a job right away but my husband was having difficulty. We decided to buy a small business. I trusted his decision and gave him my total support. The business seemed good for him. At the same time we both realized it was taking a lot of his time. Our time together became less and less. The business had become first priority. After a month or so, my husband decided we would make Friday night "our "night.

After thirty five years of marriage I still loved my husband. Our love I thought was stronger than ever. I felt special, loved, and secure with him. He was still a romantic. I can remember cooking in the kitchen, and he pulled me away to dance to a song that was playing on the radio. I loved this man. We had our struggles but I thought our trials made us stronger. Nothing could ever come between us.

After arriving home I followed my usual routine of checking the mail, sorting it, and removing my work shoes. I hurriedly changed into shorts and a tank top, and poured me a glass of cold lemonade. I sat down in my chair to relax for a few minutes. It felt good to sit and do nothing. It had been a busy week at work but Friday had finally arrived, and it had become my favorite day of the week. My husband and I would go out to dinner just the two of us. We would spend our time talking, laughing, but no business. We were never in a rush to order dinner. Time for me seemed to stop still and end so quickly.

This particular Friday was different. As I was getting dressed the phone rang. It was my husband calling from work. Some of his friends had stopped by the business unexpectedly. He was asking me if they could join us for dinner. I wanted to say no but I said yes. After hanging up the phone I felt disappointed. I didn't feel like sharing my husband. It was our night to spend some quality time after the long week. I continued dressing and I felt a little selfish, so I told myself there would be other Friday nights together.

We arrived at the restaurant and I greeted everyone. We sat down at our table and I went through the typical chit chat. Everyone ordered a cocktail. I conversed with the person next to me as I sipped my glass of wine. My husband sat at the other end of the table. I was there physically, but not mentally. I glanced at my husband a few times and he smiled. We had ordered our dinner but it hadn't arrived. I continued my conversation with the person next to me.

Time to me was moving slowly. I remembered how his friends had been drinking before arriving at the restaurant. My husband as well, I thought, had been drinking too much. They were all acting silly and telling jokes. I pretended like I understood but I didn't, and I felt bored. I was ready for the evening to end. I looked away and thought of other things.

It wasn't long after I noticed a very unpleasant scene. I saw my husband looking at someone in an intimate way, in the same way he often looked at me. Immediately I turned away and denied the image to myself. I continued trying to converse with one of his friends, but my mind kept going back to that disturbing image I had just seen. I glanced toward my husband again, and this time they were both eyeing each other like two lovers. I couldn't believe what I was seeing. This can't be true I told myself. Yet at the same time I felt sick to my stomach. My legs felt weak. I wanted to run but I couldn't move. My legs felt like rubber. Somehow I managed to get up and go outside thinking the air outside might help. I was wrong! It was hot outside. I felt faint. My thoughts kept going back to what I had just witnessed.

"God", I called out within, "what is happening here?" Suddenly my husband appeared looking very concerned. He thought I was feeling sick. "Let me get you a wet towel," he said to me.

I just stared at him for a moment and then I answered him. I told Him I didn't need a towel. He thought maybe I was sick from the wine. I said I felt sick but it wasn't from what I was drinking but from what I had just witnessed. At first he was silent and then he made a move toward me. He was getting closer to me. I was feeling uneasy. He was telling me I was imagining things. He wanted to kiss me and I pulled away. I did not want him to touch me.

"There is something going on here and I want an explanation." I told him. Again he denied any wrong doing, but I continued to demand the truth and he finally shook his head yes. "Take me home," I told him. "Tell your friends whatever and let's go." As I waited for him, my insides felt achy and tears began to just pour down my cheeks. "God", again my insides cried out. "Please tell me this is not true."

We rode all the way home in silence. After arriving home I told him to go to bed. "We need to discuss this issue tomorrow when you're sober." He didn't respond. I had forgotten he had to work the next day for half a day. We also had a prior social commitment the next evening. I hardly slept that night. I tossed and turned. I cried. I would replay the dreadful scene over and over in my mind. Maybe he was right that I had over reacted. I don't remember falling asleep, or hearing my husband leaving in the morning.

The next morning I woke up with tired puffy eyes. The entire night before kept haunting my mind. I tried to analyze and toss the thoughts away. It wasn't happening. I stayed in my pajamas most of the day. I wouldn't answer the phone. I don't remember doing anything. I would cry one minute and pray the next.

Afternoon came and I bathed and dressed. My husband arrived home and didn't say much. "I'll hurry so we can leave for the party, "he said. It was a quiet drive to our friend's house. He tried to make conversation about his day. I just nodded. I was polite but not myself at the party. We both had a cocktail and chatted with friends. I was so ready to leave and continue our conversation about the previous night. So, I finally gave my husband the signal that it was time to say good night. On our way home he talked about the party that we just attended.

I was quiet and dreading the upcoming discussion about the previous night. We arrived home and then he asked me if I wanted to go out on the town. I couldn't believe what I was hearing. It was as if all was okay and like nothing had happened the night before. I was stunned. I thought to myself does he think I'm just going to pretend like nothing happened. I looked at him with a stern face and asked him to sit down. "We need to talk about last night" I said. He sat down and one more time he said, "last night was nothing". I couldn't believe his reply. I reminded him of the scene. He looked at me confused.

I was getting upset and outraged. I kept on and on. He finally said the words, which would change my life forever. Softly he said, "I'm gay . . ." "You are what?" I said, crying. He repeated he was gay. "What?" I said in disbelief, "how long?" My voice trembled? "All my life," he answered. All of a sudden I felt out of control. My whole body was shaking. My heart was pounding and my head felt heavy like it was going to burst. My legs were weak. I felt faint, stunned, and shocked all at the same time. My breathing became heavy.

I wanted to shout or scream but no words came out of my mouth. I couldn't move. I wanted to cry out but I was speechless. I felt numb. Dead. I felt as if I was caught in a hurricane with no way out. I felt all kind of feelings. I felt betrayed, hurt, and ignorant. How did I not know? "God, where are you?" I questioned. I just sat there and he did too without saying a word. It seemed like hours when I finally burst and all I could say was, "Oh God, Oh God." He said nothing.

I don't remember when we went to bed that night. We were both silent. I was exhausted. I know he slept in my youngest son's room. At one point I thought I had entered the twilight zone. This can't be real. It was like a bad dream but I was awake. Our family life had divided. What was next? I felt scared. "Oh God, tell me my husband is not gay." Time moved on slowly.

Chapter 5

AFTER THE DISASTER

We continued to live in the same house in separate bedrooms. We put the house up for sale. "Who was this man?" I'd ask myself. I refused to tell our children that their father was gay. I just couldn't tell them. My God I could hardly say it to myself. At first my husband refused to tell our children he was gay. He kept telling me we would work out this situation. He finally told our children after much discussion. It was all so upsetting. I had to face more drama.

One by one he told our three children he was gay. First our daughter, the peacemaker, seemed to have handled it well. The question was had she really handled it, or was she in denial like me? Our youngest son cried and cried. He had questions for his dad but no reply from him. All I could do was hold him in my arms to try and console him. I felt a loss for words. I saw his pain and as a mother I felt helpless.

Last he told our oldest son. His reaction was the worst. I will never forget the expression on his face of disbelief. It went from confusion, pain, and then anger. I finally had to tell him to please leave before the evening ended in disaster. I couldn't fix his pain or anyone's pain. My life around me was literally falling apart and I couldn't do anything but pray. Once again my childhood came back to haunt me. My children were now caught in the middle. I was faced to see their pain but was unable to do anything. I felt helpless.

My husband kept telling me we were going to work things out. I wanted to believe him. For a moment in my mind I thought I could. I was bargaining. I tried God I wanted to believe him. One day he came home and I was on the floor just crying hysterically. "I want my life back!" I kept saying those words over and over. He held me until I calmed down. "It's going to be okay," he said. It was never okay again.

So many mixed feelings. Where do I go or who can help me? My life seemed so unstable. I definitely was lost. We sold the house and went to separate apartments. I continued to work and he handled our business. I was still in denial. I was trying to adjust to being on my own, but not doing very well. Everywhere I turned I was stumbling.

I remember the first time I went to the grocery store. I walked around and couldn't make a decision of what to buy. I kept remembering shopping for two. I knew what my husband liked but I didn't know what I wanted to eat. I felt alone and scared. Tears came to my eyes. I was frustrated. I left the grocery store empty handed. I couldn't make a decision.

I wasn't functioning well at my job. I was still in contact with my husband. A part of me couldn't let go. I kept hoping our relationship would survive. I went to see our pastor. He was no help. I felt more confused, and upset when I left. I was angry at God. I thought I had been a good Christian. I was a good mother, a good wife. What was happening?

Chapter 6

REALIZATION

My husband and I would sometimes see each other at my apartment. We ate dinner and talked. Hope continued for me. I began to read material about homosexuals. I wanted to understand, but the more I read about it, the more confused I became. This is not my husband.

I was so much in denial. I read about aids and HIV. I recalled a family we knew who had lost a son to aids. It had been a rough time for them. I read a section about sex. I was shocked. I felt disgusted. Where have I been? Surely this does not apply to my husband. He would never have sex with another man. We had an active sex life. Surely I would have known. I was going to discuss this issue with him the next time we'd met. Certainly he will assure me this was not true.

During this time I was having trouble eating and sleeping. I was losing weight, drinking more than one glass of wine, and thinking it would help with my pain. We finally met to discuss our business. The entire time my mind wandered off to the topic on sex. I couldn't wait to discuss it. After finishing "shop talk" I brought up the "sex subject" to him. I just came out and asked,

"Have you had sex with other men?" He didn't answer. I wanted to hear the word no but he never answered. I knew then he had. I started to cry and yell. "How could you?" "What were you thinking?" "I thought you loved me". "What about my health?" He replied that he was cautious. "Did you forget to mention it to me?" "I can't believe you could do this to me."

I stood up hysterically and demanded him to leave. I felt betrayed again. He left. I poured me a glass of wine and then another one. I wanted to stop my pain. I wept and wept. I wanted to die. I called out to God. My world was falling apart around me. I didn't know how much more I could handle. I had no control. I faced the truth. I hurt so badly. I felt defeated. My marriage was over. It was downhill after that. I went to the hospital three times and was finally diagnosed with anxiety attacks.

Chapter 7

DEPRESSION

I continued losing weight, not sleeping, and drinking. It was like I had fallen in a hole and couldn't crawl out. Everything around me was dark. "Who cares?" I had entered into the stage of depression.

I was a burden to everyone. My children and my friends. I'm sure they were all tired of listening to me. I was tired of me. I felt deserted by God. I felt disconnected. I didn't know where I belonged anymore? Where to turn? I thought about ending my life. I went to bed planning how to end it all. I was hurting so bad inside. The void inside was getting worse. I felt so empty and alone. I would think in bed about my life before and how it was over now. I felt useless and hopeless. I reached a dead end. I wanted to stop the feelings of pain. I wanted to die.

I felt confused and abandoned. I came so close to ending my life. When I remembered calling out to my deceased grandmother and to God so desperately. Something at that moment touched me inside. I felt cold and then warmth came over me. I felt safe. It was like someone was comforting me. I knew God was with me. My grandmother's voice echoed from the past saying, "You can make it." "You are not alone." I sat up in bed and yelled repeatedly, "I'm not alone". "I want to live, God". I want to see my only grandson grow up. I kept picturing my grandson in my mind. I kept telling myself repeatedly I want to live Lord.

At some point I fell asleep. I woke up the next morning with my head feeling lighter and clearer. "I'm going to make it" I said, to myself. I started praying and said my rosary. I was thinking of ways to help my situation. I read verses from the bible for consolation. Psalm 23:4 even though I walk in the dark valley I fear no evil; for you are at my side with your rod and your staff that give me courage.

I looked into possible retreats and ways to get better. It was a huge step for me. I knew I had a long road ahead of me, but I was willing to try. God was with me.

Chapter 8

CHALLENGE

I had no idea how bumpy the road ahead would be. The first challenge was getting tested for HIV. How uncomfortable I felt. I felt dirty. The questions I had to answer were humiliating. I felt awkward. In my mind I thought everyone knew. I wanted to leave when the nurse called my name. I almost left, but I knew leaving was not the answer. The test was negative but I had to be checked again in six months. Just what I need to hear.

Was there no end? I decided to file for divorce. Doubt and mixed feelings filled my mind. What happened to the vows we made before God? Did God expect me to accept this situation? I felt lost, alone, and defeated. My life had been about marriage and family. How would I survive? I went to see another priest. He showed more compassion and gave me good advice. I felt better about my situation.

It wasn't long when I realized I knew nothing about finances. My husband always handled them. Whenever I needed more money in my account, he would take care of it. I felt completely inadequate when it came to money.

Another difficult moment I had to face was attending our courtroom hearing for divorce. Another unpleasant experience. My friend of forty years came along. How many mountains had she climbed with me? How thankful I have been for her in my life. My husband's name and mine were called before the judge.

My heart was pounding and I felt like I was going to cry, as the judge went through all the technical jargon about divorce, I whispered to God to help me to get through the moment. I didn't want my husband at that time to see me upset. Later, of course, I broke down and cried.

Chapter 9

SURVIVAL

The settling of the divorce issues was difficult and painful too. I couldn't believe my husband argued about giving me alimony. He always said he would take care of me. Suddenly money was more important. The entire divorce settlement became ugly. I soon discovered that material things were more important to him. I ended the battle. I just couldn't fight anymore. It was not only painful but also costly as well.

God will provide I told myself. He has. My journey continued. I soon discovered I wasn't comfortable with everyone. My co-workers I thought felt sorry for me. My married friends and I didn't fit in anymore. I wasn't a couple anymore. I felt lonely and bewildered. I thought my marriage would be different, not like my parents. After much discernment and prayer, I decided to make a weekend for widowed, divorced, or singles. I didn't know which above category to check. "Where do I fit in?" I was hesitant and scared to face the weekend.

The week before I almost canceled. I remember my daughter encouraging me to attend. "Mom, if you don't try, you are going to drown." "Please try", she said. So there I was making this weekend about which I knew nothing. I didn't know anyone as well. The weekend was difficult for me. After one of the talks I fell apart crying hysterically. I told the retreat leaders I was not supposed to be there. I just wanted to have the life I once lived.

Finally a gentle, old hand touched me and asked me to go with her. I went to her room and I continued to cry, and she consoled me. I found out later that she was the Spiritual Director and therapist for the retreat. The weekend did help me to deal with some inner feelings. I met other people with different problems who were hurting as well.

I came away with hope. I became involved with the ministry. In helping others I was helping myself. I was finally able to admit, "Oh God, my husband is gay." I became very close to Sister Mary. She counseled me and led me on the right road to recovery. Sister Mary became my spiritual advisor and friend. She showed me how to live in the present. I had been dwelling on the past and worried about the future. When I awake in the mornings now, I remind myself I only have today. It helps me to start my day in a better frame of mind. I still have my not so good days, but I work at being positive.

My mother passed away that same year. More feelings to face. I finally let go of my denial and grief. God kept pushing me. I was beginning to find myself. My self esteem was coming back. I was a good person. I did not cause this break up in my marriage; although there had been times I thought maybe I had contributed to my husband's lifestyle. Maybe I wasn't such a good wife? I tortured myself with ifs and buts.

I dealt with some anger too. I wanted him to hurt like me. I wanted to shake him over and over. I thought maybe he would come to his senses, and admit he made a mistake. I stopped by at our place of business unexpectedly, and he was entertaining some of his gay friends. He went from laughing with his friends to being uncomfortable because I was there. We managed to get into an argument. He wasn't good at confrontations. He stormed out as I continued to call him a coward. We were both acting like children. I did have thoughts of revenge but I didn't know how. All that kept crossing my mind was the effect it was having on our children. Did he not care?

I continued to struggle with mixed feelings. Sometimes I thought God had forgotten and abandoned me. Would I ever get over these difficult times in my life? I continued to pray and attend mass. Many times my mind would just wander. I would think about how my life was so simple at one time. Now everywhere I turned there was turmoil. I continued to function at work.

I tried attending meetings in the evenings. Staying busy was good. It kept my mind off my troubles. I had good friends that would come over or we do lunch. How blessed I was to have them and still do.

Night time was my worst enemy. I didn't like being alone. I often would think of the past. I would go to bed and I tossed and turned. Sometimes I reached for my husband but he wasn't there. I'd cry and cry. Other times I would awake frightened. I often called my friend in the middle of the night. I'd called on God many times too. So many questions but no answers.

I felt at times like I was caught in a trap. I just couldn't get out. My feelings were up and down like being on a roller coaster. Some days better, other days worse. I had a prayer I would say often to God. "God, I don't know where I'm going, I don't see the road ahead of me. I do know you will be with me." It was true that God did not leave me. I had survived.

Now I was divorced and that word described my life. Divorce. It was not suppose to happen to me. I thought my life was going to be different compared to my parents. I thought we would grow old together and do all the things about which we had once talked and dreamed. I continued to function and make the best of my life. I had to keep trying.

My single friends asked me to join them in the night life. I soon found out it was not for me. I felt uncomfortable. I joined a church singles group. We would go to movies, dinner, and church dances. I met a nice man at one of the dances and he asked me out to dinner. I said yes. I entered the world of dating. My first date I felt uneasy. I felt like it was wrong like cheating. My date was a gentleman and could sense my nervousness. He was polite and kept the conversation simple.

Chapter 10

NEW LIFE AND FORGIVENESS

I moved to another town where my daughter lived. It was another uncertain road, another change, a different city and new job. I was missing my friends. On the other hand, I was close to my daughter and grandchildren. My grandchildren were a blessing, a joy, and a tremendous part of my growth. They loved me unconditionally. They filled my void. They were my strength and my reasons to keep fighting to live.

I still was not at peace. A part of me felt like I was torn, uneasy, and restless. At times I was bitter too. One of my struggles was forgiveness. I felt resentful. "Why did you do this to me?" "You abandoned me." It was a constant battle for me. At times I wanted my husband to hurt like me. There was turmoil inside of me. He never told me he was sorry. Why? He seemed to be doing well with his new life. I often wondered if he missed me. Yet for me there wasn't a day that passed that I didn't think of him. People would tell me it was time to be over my loss.

It wasn't so easy. I told myself they had not experienced what I had gone through. How could they understand? I asked God to help me forget and tell me how to stop loving someone after thirty-five years. I kept reading my bible. I read repeatedly the Prodigal Son story. I had to somehow forgive my ex-husband.

I couldn't continue reopening this wound. It would never heal. I just wrestled with the idea. Forgiveness came unannounced one day. I had been meditating and praying about the times God had forgiven me. I thought about how God had always forgiven others. He had forgiven the men who crucified him! How could I not forgive? It wasn't easy but I forgave my husband. I even called him to tell him I forgave him. He responded like it wasn't a big deal. It was to me. I surrendered to God that day. I let God do his will. I quit fighting myself. I let God help me. It wasn't easy, but I felt like a heavy burden was lifted off my shoulders. I reached acceptance. I thought I was in control of my life but I wasn't.

Still at times I want to be in control, and then I realize I'm not, and my day goes better. I see my ex-husband at family functions sometimes. We are cordial. I still miss him sometimes. I think about how it could have been, especially when I'm with our grandchildren. I pray for him. I believe the life he's living is wrong in God's eyes. Whoever said life was supposed to be easy was mistaken.

Another step I took that helped me heal was getting an annulment. Annulment in the Catholic Church is a procedure which determines should the marriage be void or not. The Catholic Church believes that when a man and woman unite in the church they receive the sacrament of marriage. As I believe as well. A sacrament is a outward sign of grace in our faith. Because I am Catholic it was important to me to work on getting my annulment. I have to admit it was difficult at first having to answer some of the questions reliving times in my marriage again. I didn't want to at first but I did. The results in the end were good for me. Writing about my marriage helped me. I was able to have closure. Another chapter ended.

The following year I did get my annulment. I continued on my path with faith and hope. I hit another roadblock. I was having health problems and went through a period of not knowing what was wrong. It took a while before I was diagnosed with multiple sclerosis. It was another time of trial and adjustment. I was relieved to know what was wrong with me but faced another mountain to climb. I felt let down. I had another decision regarding treatment and learning about multiple sclerosis. My first reaction was worry and shocked. Why? God, I said, "what next?"

The next few months were about facing challenges and changes in my life. There was more testing and decisions to be made. It was not the worst acceptance I had to face. I finally gave it to the Lord and kept fighting. Through the months ahead I learned I was a survivor. I was not going to throw in the towel. No giving up for me.

Chapter 11

ACCEPTANCE

I had reached acceptance in life with my marriage and illness. "Thank you, God, for not giving up on me."

It has been almost twelve years since that hot, summer day. It has been a long journey and sometimes I thought I wasn't going to make it but I did. "Yes, I have." I spend time with my grandchildren and I realize how precious they are to me. They give me joy and happiness. I now have four grandsons and one granddaughter. I feel grateful and blessed to be a part of their lives. I think of my angelic grandmother and I hope I'm a good example to my grandchildren like she was to me. I miss my grandmother but I know she watches over me. I'm blessed to have a job I enjoy. I took a risk at trying a new occupation, and it has been a positive move for me.

Life is precious and I try not to take it for granted. It does sadden me at times when I think of the loss of a marriage and the family division it cost. A part of me will always love the man I married and thought I knew.

I have been receptive to love again. I continue to pray and ask God to guide me. I know I can take care of myself. I have found my dignity. I don't need a man to take care of me. The only man I really need is God Almighty. I did pray to God to send me a Christian man and he did. We enjoy each other's company, but marriage is not in the picture for now.

I may not always understand the why in my life, but I know God has a reason and a plan for me. My plan is to work with gay spouses and help them. It is one of the reasons I'm writing this book. It would have been helpful for me if I had known someone with a gay spouse, or known someone I could have related or talked to about my experience.

I have learned so many important lessons, and I continue to empathize with the gay spouse. We may have different stories, but our feelings have been the same at one time or another.

I hope my story has been helpful and enlightening in some small way. I repeat joyfully," thank you, God, for being there for me." "Continue to strengthen me and guide me to do your will."